December 1988
To Sarah
Merry Christmas
Mommy &
Daddy

Harold Roth's Big Book of

HORSES

Text by Margo Lundell

Grosset & Dunlap • New York

To Robin, Alexis, and Danielle — my fillies.   H.R.

Photographs copyright © 1987 by Harold Roth. Text copyright © 1987 by Margo Lundell.
All rights reserved. Published by Grosset & Dunlap, a member of The Putnam Publishing Group, New York.
Published simultaneously in Canada. Printed in Italy. Library of Congress Catalog Card Number: 86-82560
ISBN 0-448-19203-9

Special thanks to: Kay Coyte, technical editor
                    Bonnie Silver (A Day in the Life of a Young Horse Owner)
                    Jamie Moore and the Ox-Ridge Hunt Club (Young Show Riders)

All photographs are the property of Equine Images Inc. except for photographs
provided by All-Sport Vandystadt, page 39; Katey Barrett, page 44; Joseph
DiOrio, pages 9, 15, 17 (bottom), 24; Douglas Lees, pages 30, 36, 37, 45;
and The Royal Canadian Mounted Police, page 40.

Reinforced Binding   A B C D E F G H I J

Introduction

Of all the animals in creation, the horse is the perfect combination of strength, intelligence, speed, and beauty. Only a horse can pull a plow, run a race, and please an audience with its graceful form.

In this century, horses do not have to work as hard as they once did. Tractors have taken their place on the farm. Tanks have replaced them on the battlefield. We travel by car, plane, and train rather than by horse.

More than ever before, however, we now enjoy horses for sport and pleasure. Thousands of horse shows and rodeos take place in the United States each year. Crowds of people flock to race tracks daily. In all, there are nine million horses in this country today, and the number is growing.

Horses are not being forgotten in the age of technology. For many people, young and old, riders and spectators, there is a fascination and love for horses that will always endure.

How Horses Grow

◄ A **foal** is a newborn male or female horse. Born in the early spring, a foal weighs about 100 pounds at birth, most of which is legs. Within minutes of birth, a foal stands up, wobbles a few steps to its mother, and begins to nurse.

A male foal is called a colt. A female is called a filly. Colts and fillies spend their first six months close to their mothers. At about six months, they are weaned and are then called weanlings.

◄ A **yearling** is a one-year-old. The colts and fillies that will be race horses all celebrate their first birthday on January 1st of the year after their birth, no matter when they were born.

Yearlings are happy, frisky creatures. At one year, they are about half as big as adult horses. They still have the rough coats they were born with. When the animals are two years old their coats will be smooth and fine.

◄ A **two-year-old** horse is like a teenager. It has almost reached its full height, but its muscles and bones are not fully developed. In the second year of life, young race horses are trained to compete at the track. By the time they are two, they are ready to run.

Horses are considered fully grown when they are five. At that age, a colt is called a horse. For breeding purposes, he is referred to as a stallion. A filly grows up to be a mare.

The Body of a Horse

Forelock, Forehead, Muzzle, Cheek, Neck, Chest, Elbow, Forearm, Knee, Cannon, Pastern, Hoof, Fetlock, Mane, Shoulder, Withers, Back, Loin, Flank, Croup, Dock, Rump, Belly, Barrel, Stifle, Gaskin, Thigh, Tail, Hock

Horses are large animals. A big draft horse (a work horse) can weigh 2,000 pounds. Light saddle horses usually weigh close to 1,000 pounds. Ponies can weigh as little as 300 pounds.

The height of a horse is measured in hands. For centuries men used their hands to describe a horse's height. A hand equals four inches, about the width of a human hand. Horses are measured from the ground up to the top of the withers, the highest part of the shoulders. A horse that stands 15 hands is 60 inches tall.

Most horses live for more than 20 years, and some spend useful lives into their thirties.

Breeding Farms

A breeding farm is a place where special breeds or kinds of horses are raised. A farm may be large, with well cared-for barns and hundreds of acres of rolling pastures. A big staff is needed to run one of these farms, including stable managers, trainers, grooms, exercise riders, and others.

Horse owners with mares to breed may buy the services of a stud from the farm. A stud is a stallion used for breeding. A valuable stallion can earn millions of dollars in stud fees.

Breeding farms help meet the demand for certain popular horse breeds, such as Arabian, Thoroughbred, or Morgan. Fine mares and stallions are bred on the farm. Their foals are born eleven months later and may be sold as yearlings to interested buyers.

There are many other ways to buy a horse. Some people go to professional horse dealers. Others buy a horse in a claiming race at the track. A less formal method is to check listings in horse magazines or local newspapers.

Horses are also sold at auctions—a sale in which a horse goes to the highest bidder. One of the most famous yearling auctions is held during August each year in Saratoga Springs, New York. The handsome young race horses offered at that auction all have fine conformation, or physical features, and well-known sires and dams (fathers and mothers). An excellent colt will sell for more than one million dollars.

Breeds

No one kind of horse suits everyone's needs. As a result, many different breeds have been developed over the centuries. Some breeds are especially fast. Others are strong. A particular breed may be known for its stamina or grace.

Purebreds, also known as thoroughbreds (not the breed), are horses with ancestors in the same breed for several generations. A registered horse is usually a purebred. When it was born it was officially listed, or registered, with the association representing its breed.

◀ An **Arabian** is one of the oldest known breeds. Born in the desert and bred by Bedouin tribesmen, Arabian horses are famous for their beauty, speed, and outstanding endurance.

American Saddlebreds (not shown) are tall, graceful creatures known as the "peacocks of the show ring." They can learn and perform five gaits, or ways of moving, instead of the normal three.

◀ **Thoroughbreds** (the breed) are the elegant, fast aristocrats of the race track. Every Thoroughbred can trace its ancestry back to one of three Arabian stallions imported to England about 300 years ago.

◄ The **Morgan** is named for a legendary Vermont stallion whose owner was Justin Morgan. Morgans are both handsome and sturdy. They can pull heavy loads or run a fast race with equal ease.

◄ **Standardbreds** are the finest harness racers in the world. Originally bred to pull carriages smoothly, these fast-stepping trotters and pacers tend to be calmer than Thoroughbred racers.

◄ **Tennessee Walking Horses** were developed by Southern plantation owners to ride while overseeing their vast lands. Front feet lifting high, these stylish horses are known for their fast, smooth "running walk."

◀ The **American Quarter Horse** is the classic workhorse of the western range. It is also the most popular breed in America today. The horse's name comes from the fact that it can run a quarter-mile race faster than any other horse.

◀ **Color Breeds:** Horses of one breed are not always the same color. An Arabian, for example, can be black, white, or brown. There are some colorful horses, however, that are classed in color breeds. Spotted **Appaloosas** (shown left) and golden **palominos** are in that category.

◀ **Ponies** are not young horses. They belong to special breeds of small horses. To qualify as a pony, the animal must be no taller than 14.2 hands. **Shetlands** are the smallest of the many breeds of ponies. Stocky and barrel-shaped, they look like miniature draft horses. **Welsh ponies** (not shown) look like small Arabians. They are taller than Shetlands, and many young riders graduate to Welsh ponies when they have outgrown Shetlands.

Color

Special terms are used to describe horses of a certain color. For example, a dun is a yellowish-gray horse. A chestnut is reddish-brown. A bay is brown with black "points," meaning its mane, tail, and lower legs. A gray horse is called a gray, but its coat is actually a mixture of black and white hairs. There are many other names for a horse's color.

Many horses have markings, or white patterns, on their faces or legs. There are also names for these markings. A star is a white patch on the forehead, for instance. A stocking is a white leg mark from the hoof to the knee.

Senses

Horses have the largest eyes of any land animal except the ostrich. The eyes move independently: a horse can look forward with one eye and back with the other. Horses have keen hearing and can move their ears in the direction of a sound to hear it more clearly. Their well-developed sense of smell helps them pick up scents from far away.

As for taste, horses have a sweet tooth and love molasses as well as sugar. The metal bit that fits into their mouths when they are bridled does not interfere with their sense of taste. The bit rests over the tongue in an empty space between the horse's teeth.

Disposition

Horses seem to have a sense of humor. A certain horse whinny even sounds like laughter. Horses can also become angry. If the ears are flattened back against the head, it's usually a sign of anger.

A horse's individual temperament depends partly on its breed and partly on its early training. However, all horses are known for having a good memory and for being able to learn through repetition. They are herd animals with an instinct to obey a leader. This instinct makes a horse willing to obey a rider or trainer.

What Horses Like to Do

Horses run for the pure joy of it. Released into a pasture, a colt will suddenly race across a meadow as if thrilled with its freedom. Older horses, too, will jump and play and kick up their heels. Mares will gallop ahead of their foals, as if gently challenging them to a race.

Horses love to eat. They are grazing animals and like to eat a little at a time all through the day. With its incisors, the cutting teeth at the front of its mouth, a horse bites off grass close to the ground. With its molars, the grinding teeth at the back, the horse chews the grass slowly and carefully.

Horses are happy when they can roll on the ground, on grass, in sand, or in dirt. They will not usually choose to roll in mud, but they seem to know that a slight coating of dirt sometimes helps keep insects from biting.

Horses often rub themselves against trees or fence posts. Rubbing and scratching seem to feel good. However, horses are ticklish and sensitive in places. If groomed too hard over their ribs and belly, for example, they will stamp the ground and even kick. A horse has a particularly soft nose and upper lip.

Horses sleep standing up. A strong muscle in the horse's neck keeps its head from dropping down completely. The leg joints lock while a horse sleeps so that its legs don't buckle. Horses sometimes lie down in their stalls for short periods. Lying down takes the weight of a horse's body off its delicate legs.

A Day in the Life of a Young

Bonnie is a ten-year-old who lives on a farm in New England. She has a pony named Bambi who keeps her very busy.

Early in the morning, Bonnie goes to the stable to take care of Bambi, her gray pony. Bambi sticks his head out over the top of the Dutch doors to his stall. Bonnie gives him a pat on the nose and a handful of fresh grass. Then she goes into the stall.

Bambi stays out of the way while Bonnie mucks out, or cleans, the stall. She uses a long-handled pitchfork to pick up wet or dirty sawdust and dumps it in a bin. The bin will be hauled to the manure pile. Then Bonnie will put down fresh sawdust. A thick layer of straw or sawdust is easier for Bambi to stand on than the hard floor alone.

Horse Owner

Bonnie brings fresh water. Bambi wants a drink before Bonnie can get the bucket into the stall. Bonnie also brings fresh hay and oats for Bambi's breakfast.

Horses drink a lot of water, up to 10 or 12 gallons a day. They eat a lot too, as much as 15 to 20 pounds of hay plus several quarts of oats or other grains.

Later in the morning, Bonnie puts on her jodhpurs, or riding pants. But before she goes riding, Bonnie has to groom Bambi.

Bonnie puts a halter and lead line on Bambi and ties him to a fence. Then she uses a hard rubber currycomb on Bambi's coat to loosen the dirt and matted hair. She sweeps the dirt off with a grooming brush.

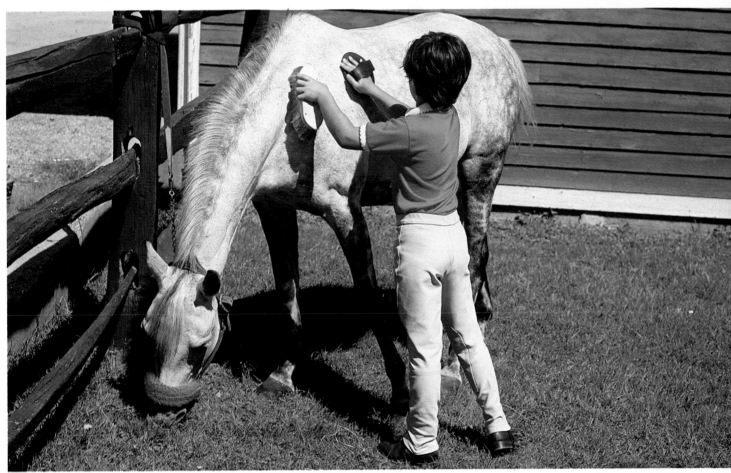

Before and after each ride, Bonnie has to scrape out the dirt and stones in Bambi's hoofs. If she didn't, Bambi might develop sore places or an infection. Bonnie uses a hoof pick to do this. She is careful not to hurt the soft center of the hoof called the frog.

It's time to saddle up. First Bonnie puts a pad on Bambi's back so that the saddle will not rub against his skin. Then she places the saddle on his back and tightens the girth, which is the strap that goes under Bambi's belly. Bonnie uses an English riding saddle—smaller and lighter than a Western saddle.

At last Bonnie and her pony are free to ride. The green pastures are long and inviting. The grass flies by as Bambi runs the length of the meadow.

To control Bambi, Bonnie uses what riders call "aids." Aids include voice signals, the use of a riding crop, or whip, and signals from the rider's hands, legs, or shifting body weight. Hand signals must be very light. As a rider pulls on the reins, the horse feels pressure on the metal bit in his mouth. A horse's mouth is sensitive. If the rider yanks on the reins over and over, the horse will develop what is known as a hard, or unresponsive mouth.

As for leg signals, horses are trained to turn "away from the leg." When the rider presses his or her left leg, the horse will go to the right. Pressure from the right leg makes the horse go left. Hand signals are the opposite. Horses are trained to turn <u>toward</u> the hand. For example, when the rider pulls on the right rein, the horse turns right.

After the ride, Bonnie helps Bambi cool off by hosing him down. A shower also rinses off any sweat. Bambi likes his shower, but Bonnie can only give him one when the weather is warm.

Several times a year Bambi gets a real bath. Bonnie puts soap on a sponge and scrubs Bambi from head to toe. Then she must rinse him off well because leftover soap could irritate his skin.

In the afternoon, Bonnie turns Bambi out. This means she releases him into a meadow or pasture. On this day Bambi is grazing behind the barn. Being outdoors gives Bambi fresh air, sunlight, and exercise, too. While he is out, Bambi does not wear a bridle. A bridle is the leather and metal harness that fits over a horse's head.

While Bambi is turned out, Bonnie cleans the tack or riding equipment. To do this, she rubs a damp sponge on saddle soap. Then she rubs the waxy soap into the bridle and saddle. Saddle soap keeps the leather supple and soft so that it won't crack or break. When she's finished, Bonnie puts the tack back in the barn.

Late in the day, Bonnie brings Bambi back into the stable. When he is in his stall, Bonnie will give Bambi his dinner—more hay and oats and fresh water. Then Bambi will sleep in his stall, waking up from time to time to eat some hay. The familiar sounds of other horses in nearby stalls will lull him to sleep again. ▪

The Blacksmith
A blacksmith, or farrier, is the person who takes care of a horse's feet. Most blacksmiths travel from farm to farm, carrying their portable anvil, hammers, rasps, and other tools with them.

A horse's hoofs are like human fingernails and grow a little all the time. A blacksmith must file down the hoofs every six to eight weeks. He also nails new shoes on a horse when the old ones are worn. There are no nerves in the hard tissue of a hoof so that a horse feels no pain when it is shod. Horseshoes are made of light metal nowadays and do not need to be heated in order to be shaped. The most lightweight shoes of all are worn by race horses.

The Veterinarian

Some veterinarians, or animal doctors, specialize in taking care of horses. Like blacksmiths, they travel to individual farms or stables when called.

Horses need checkups at least once a year. During a checkup, the animal will receive shots to prevent various diseases. The vet may give the horse medicine to get rid of worms in its stomach. He or she may also float, or file down, the horse's molars, which will grow all through the animal's life. When a horse is lame or ill, the veterinarian will come and diagnose the problem. In special cases, a sick horse may be taken to an equine, or horse, hospital. One simple operation that a veterinarian can perform right in the stable is gelding. When a male horse is gelded, certain parts of its reproductive system are removed.

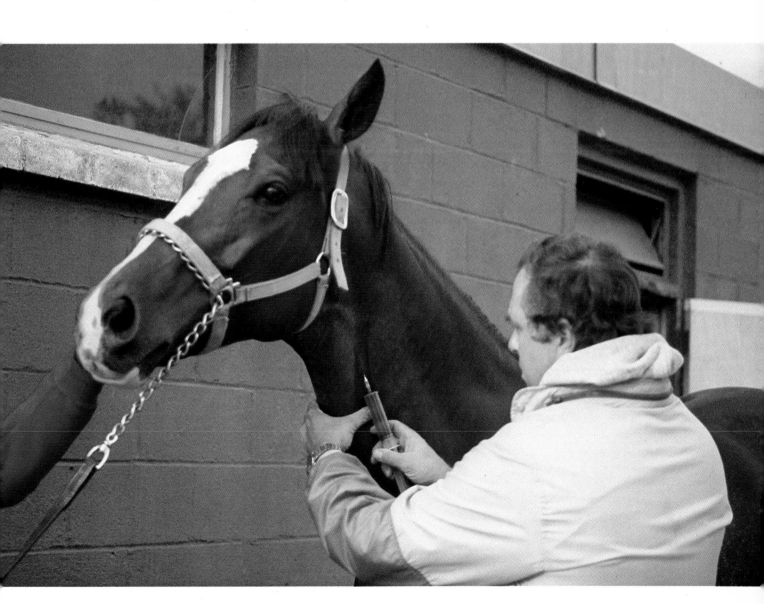

Young Show Riders

There are more than 5,000 horse shows eacn year in the United States and Canada. Some are limited to adult riders but many include junior classes for young riders.

To compete, a rider may have to ship his or her horse by van or trailer to the show grounds. Some horses need a lot of patient coaxing to get them into a van. Others are known as scramblers, which means they have trouble staying on their feet once the trailer is moving.

Arriving at the show or fair may be the start of a week of competition or just a day of contests. During the show, the rider may stable the horse in its trailer or rent stall space in a tent set up near the show ring.

Keeping a horse calm and well-groomed before a show can be hard work. Many horses become over-excited by the strange new scents and sounds around them.

"Walk, please," says the judge, and the young riders in their equitation, or showmanship class, press their horses forward into a walk, the first of the horse's three gaits. The second is trot. The third and fastest is canter. Galloping is often considered a fast canter.

Young show riders may jump their horses over low fences. The goal in most jumping classes is to clear the obstacle without touching it. Style does not count, and a rider may compete on any breed of horse or pony. Jumping takes a great deal of practice but is probably the most exciting of all show events.

Six ribbons are usually awarded to the winners in a particular class. First place is blue, of course. Second is red. Yellow is third. Fourth is white. Fifth is pink, and a sixth place ribbon is green. In some shows, a rider may win a silver trophy or plate or cup. A few shows award fancy blankets to the winning horses.

Advanced Competition

A rider who is making a career out of showing may compete nearly all year long. Traveling from a home stable, the show rider may perform locally or in large, statewide events, in huge national shows or in major international competition, such as the Olympic Games.

In advanced show jumping, the fences and obstacles are very high. The performers are often timed. Expected to perform with speed, daring, and precision, the horses and riders are under a great deal of pressure. Show scoring is done by a system of penalty points known as faults. A rider's mount, or horse, may receive four faults, for example, for knocking down a rail. The highest jump in show competition is called the "Great Wall." The jump is often more than seven feet high.

In dressage competition, a highly exact and elegant series of movements must be performed. Horses trained in dressage are the most skilled of all. The rider seems to give no signal to the horse, but the animal is in fact obeying extremely slight leg pressures or a shifting of weight by the rider. The horses obey instantly and perform with pure grace.

Eventing is a strenuous three-day form of competition. Growing in popularity, eventing is based on the hard training and exercises once given to cavalry horses. The first day is dressage competition. The second is an exhausting cross-country race that can be more than ten miles long. The course is filled with hedges to jump and streams to cross. On the third day, a jumping competition is held in a show stadium.

Following the Hounds

Fox hunting is an old tradition in England and in some parts of America, too. The members of a hunt club, properly dressed and mounted, gather in the countryside on a chilly autumn day along with a pack of dogs called fox hounds. When the hounds find the scent of a fox, they begin to bay, or howl, and leap forward to follow the scent. The horses, called hunters, carry their riders after the hounds. The hunters often go at a full gallop, across fields of stubble, over stone walls, and through thick woods.

The hunt is a test of endurance for horse and rider that can sometimes last all day. Hunters must be big, courageous horses who can be relied on to jump willingly and ride evenly for hours at a time.

Playing Polo

Polo is one of the oldest games known to man. Long played in parts of Asia, the game was discovered by the British in India. Americans have adopted polo, too, and sometimes refer to it as "hockey on horseback."

The game is divided into chukkers, or periods of seven and a half minutes. There are two teams of four players each. The players use long-handled mallets to hit a wooden ball and try to drive it between the opponent's goal posts.

The strong, spirited horses used in polo are called ponies regardless of their size. They are trained to gallop forward furiously and to turn and swerve relentlessly. Their legs are protected by thick bandages or boots. A well-trained polo pony will follow the fast-moving ball almost without instructions from the rider.

Horse Racing

King Henry the Eighth of England is considered the father of racing. He was the first to keep a stable of fast horses used just for racing. Since Henry's time, horse racing has been called "the sport of kings."

Thoroughbreds dominate racing. A thousand pounds of Thoroughbred galloping around the track is a beautiful sight to see. For just a moment, all four feet under the powerful body are off the ground. The Thoroughbred's stride is huge, about two and a half times the length of its body.

Thoroughbreds are known to have great "heart," or will to win. They will run beyond their own endurance, in spite of damaged lungs or injured legs. Their heartbeat goes from a resting rate of about 30 beats

per minute up to 250 while racing. Running as fast as 40 miles per hour, the horses throw themselves into the race so completely that it takes them a quarter of a mile to slow down and come to a stop.

Racing Thoroughbreds are rewarded, however, for their fabulous efforts on the track. They are treated as the celebrities of the horse kingdom. Their babyhood is luxurious. Their early training is intense but gentle. During their racing years, which may be only a few, they are lovingly cared for by trainers, grooms, exercise riders, hot walkers, and all the people needed to coax a race horse to success. Stallions and mares with good racing records will then be retired from the track to live out their pampered lives on a breeding farm.

The Steeplechase
Steeplechasing is the sport of racing horses over obstacles. Popular in England and the eastern United States, steeplechasing got its name from country races long ago. Friends on horseback would chase each other across fields, over fences and ditches, racing toward the village church steeple in the distance.

These races are now held on oval tracks over specially built courses. The most famous, the Grand National Steeplechase near Liverpool, England, is a four-mile race over 30 obstacles. These hurdle races are exciting but sometimes dangerous. Horses swerve to avoid collisions. Jockeys can become unseated, or horses can tumble and fall. Fast Thoroughbreds are favorite mounts for these races because of the breakneck speed that is needed.

Harness Racing

Harness racing really began when horse-and-buggy drivers in earlier times challenged each other to quick races down dirt roads. Since then, it has become a major professional sport, with large purses, or prize monies, to be won. Thousands of spectators watch as handsome Standardbred horses pull special light-weight carts called sulkies around well-groomed oval tracks.

Harness racers do not gallop. They go at either a trot or a pace. Trotting means the horse's legs move in diagonal pairs. This means the front right leg and rear left leg step together. Pacers, on the other hand, step forward with front and back legs on the same side of the body. In other words, both left legs move forward together, and then both right legs. The driver sits in the sulky and controls the horse through long lines to the bridle. Pacers and trotters must be well-trained to resist the urge to gallop to the finish line.

The Cowboy's Horse

Ranchers and cowboys still round up cattle on horseback, as they have done since the West was settled. Their horses must have speed and stamina. The sturdy, muscular stock horses, or cow ponies, that they use are often not a breed but a type of horse. It may be descended in part from the Spanish horses brought to America by explorers almost four hundred years ago. A ranch horse may also be the famous American Quarter Horse.

Quarter horses, quick and strong, are described as having "cow sense," meaning an instinct for cutting, or sorting, a calf out of a herd of adult cattle or for catching a runaway steer. Quarter Horses are famous for being able to survive on sparse grass, to clamber up rugged hillsides, to swim rivers, and to brace themselves with all their might against a heavy steer thrashing at the end of a cowboy's rope.

Rodeo Competition

There are more than 500 major rodeos held every year and three times that many smaller Western-style competitions. One of the most popular of the big annual rodeos is the Calgary Stampede in Canada.

Many rough-and-tumble rodeo events demand riders with a great deal of experience. Angry Brahman bulls and semi-wild horses called broncos throw rider after rider into the dust of the ring. A favorite spectacle is calf roping. To compete, a cowboy on horseback must first lasso a running calf. Then he quickly ties the free end of the rope around the horn, or handle, of his Western saddle. The cowboy's horse must then keep the rope absolutely taut on the lassoed calf. The cowboy jumps off the horse, flips the calf to the ground, and quickly ties three of its legs together with a short rope called a "piggin' string."

Circus Horses

Ever since circuses were first started, the quiet stars of the show have been obedient and well-trained horses. Big, dependable Percherons or other draft horses have always pulled the colorful wagons and floats. Hackney horses, a light harness breed, draw the fancy parade buggies. Other horses become performers in circus acts. Two dozen at a time will obey the vocal commands of a single ringmaster as they trot through precision drills in the ring. Acrobats riding bareback depend on the horses never to alter the steady gaits they have learned.

Beautiful white Lippizaners have been called the ballet dancers of the horse kingdom. Descended from Arabian stallions and fine Spanish mares, this famous, highly intelligent, Austrian breed has been trained for centuries at the Spanish Riding School of Vienna, Austria. A performing Lippizaner stallion can leap and prance through the most beautiful and amazing series of movements ever devised for a horse.

Horses on Parade

Any dress parade, military or civil, becomes a stately spectacle when ranks of well-groomed horses and uniformed riders make their appearance. In Britain, especially, the tradition of horse guards on parade is still strong.

Months of training must be given to parade horses before they perform. Little by little, the animals are exposed to the sight of flag-waving crowds, the sounds of cheering, brass bands, police whistles, and other distractions. When the horses have learned to ignore all the hustle and bustle of a large gathering and respond only to the commands of their riders, they are ready to go on parade.

Northwest Mounties

The Royal Canadian Mounted Police is the famed federal police force in Canada. It was created in the last century to patrol the Yukon and the Northwest Territories and to keep order during the wild gold rush to the Klondike.

The Mounties no longer patrol on horseback, unfortunately. Their well-known exhibition team still exists, however, performing its impressive Musical Ride on important state occasions and in major shows. The unit's horses are specially bred, and the officers still wear their well-known wide-brimmed hats and scarlet dress tunics.

Police on Horseback

In a number of cities around the country, mounted officers and their horses make up very effective police units. They are known to prevent crime by their mere presence. A police officer on horseback can see and be seen by possible troublemakers. When half a ton of musclepower canters into an unruly crowd, people usually quiet down quickly.

New York City's "finest and tallest" are a proud mounted police unit. There is a waiting list of officers who wish to join the division. Their favorite mounts are Morgan horses and Thoroughbreds retired from the track. Stallions are rarely used for police work. Mares and geldings usually prove to be calmer and more dependable.

Horse-drawn Vehicles

Before steam energy was harnessed or combustion engines were invented, horses did most of the hard work of transporting goods and people. Draft horses were hitched to farm wagons to haul crops to market. Cavalry horses dragged heavy artillery across battlefields. There were pioneer wagons to be pulled to the West. And there were mailbags to carry, stagecoaches and streetcars to pull, boats to move along canals.

Harnessed horse teams are a rare sight now, but occasionally they can be seen. Brewery wagons are sometimes pulled ceremoniously by tall, powerful Clydesdales, a type of draft horse. In the country, farm horses are hitched to wagons so that people can go on hayrides.

A ride in a pony cart or a carriage trip through a city park is a real pleasure. There are also driving classes in some horse shows. Antique carts or carriages called surreys and gigs are brought out for the occasion, with gleaming horses guided by drivers who are called whips.

Horses used for driving are given special training. Before the pony or horse is asked to pull any weight, a trainer will spend days on foot, running behind the newly harnessed animal. Then the horse learns to drag a five- or ten-pound object. In the last phase of training, the animal is harnessed to a light, two-wheeled cart. When no longer frightened by the jolting, bouncing cart, the horse can learn to pull a heavier, four-wheeled coach.

Semi-wild Horses
Freed of the burden of harness or halter, given wide space under the sky, stallions and mares will return to their once-wild state.

In America, there are two kinds of semi-wild, or feral, horses. Feral means that a horse is the descendant of a breed that was once domesticated. Off the coast of Virginia and Maryland are the wind-blown islands of Assateague and Chincoteague. Small, wiry, untamed ponies have lived on the islands by themselves for several hundred years. They are probably descended from horses brought to this country by the early Spanish explorers.

The semi-wild horse that the American West is famous for is the mustang. It, too, has Spanish ancestors, the part-Arabian horses that Cortez and others brought here in the 1500s. A number of these horses escaped from their Spanish masters. They flourished on rich western grazing lands. Some were captured and trained by Native American peoples, but many others roamed free. By the 1800s, there were several million mustangs, living together in large bands headed by fierce stallions.

There are few mustangs left now, but some can still be found in desert canyons and valleys of the West. Today, mustangs are protected by law in the hope that their numbers will grow. Their liberty seems to symbolize the freedom of America itself.